THE CHRISTIAN HANDBOOK SERIES

Dealing with Difficult People

What is it? How should it be dealt with?
What is a Christian response?

Jocelyn Bryan

kevin mayhew

kevin mayhew

First published in Great Britain in 2009 by Kevin Mayhew Ltd
Buxhall, Stowmarket, Suffolk IP14 3BW
Tel: +44 (0) 1449 737978 Fax: +44 (0) 1449 737834
E-mail: info@kevinmayhewltd.com

www.kevinmayhew.com

9 8 7 6 5 4 3 2 1 0

ISBN 978 1 84867 121 8
Catalogue No. 1501159

Cover design by Rob Mortonson
Edited by Delian Bower and Katherine Laidler
Typeset by Richard Weaver and Chris Coe

Printed and bound in Great Britain

Contents

About the author

Jocelyn Bryan is a tutor at the Wesley Study Centre, Durham, and a Methodist local preacher. She teaches Psychology and Christian Ministry, Sexuality, Gender and Christian Ministry and some Practical Theology. Her PhD is in psychology, where she studied ageing and memory. Her research interest is in the interface between psychology, theology and Christian ministry, and she has published on adolescence. She is married and has three teenage children.

Introduction

Jocelyn Bryan and Brendan Geary

If you have picked up or bought this booklet then the chances are that you have a concern about a difficult situation in your family, workplace, church, organisation – or in your own life – and are not sure what to do about it. On the other hand, you may be in a teaching or leadership position and want to find a resource to help you with your job. Whatever has aroused your interest, it suggests that you are aware of a particular area of concern and would like to be better informed. If you come from a Christian background, you may also wonder about doing the 'right' thing in terms of your values and beliefs. This booklet, and the others in the series, have been written with you in mind.

All of us can be faced with a range of problems that do not admit to easy solutions. The complexity of our lives and the range of problems that we encounter make the task of management especially difficult. Large organisations can call on the qualified and experienced members of personnel and legal departments to assist in these situations. People in smaller organisations – small businesses, family firms, churches, schools, voluntary organisations and community projects, for example – often do not have these resources available to help deal with and navigate their way through the difficulties and competing needs and responsibilities of those involved.

This booklet is one of a series which was originally published in *The Christian handbook of abuse, addiction and difficult behaviour.* The following topics were selected as they are ones which many of us now find ourselves having to deal with, or which are regularly presented to us by the media:

- Child sexual abuse
- Partner violence
- Addiction to drugs and alcohol
- Gambling addiction
- Sexual addiction and internet pornography
- Difficult people
- Adult bullying
- Violence in the workplace.

Issues like alcohol abuse or the problems of working with 'difficult people', have been part of human experience for a long time. Some of them, however, like child abuse, adult bullying or partner violence, were not spoken about, and society, families, churches and organisations colluded in denying that they existed. The problems of internet pornography are a new manifestation of an old problem, but the ease of access of the internet has led to this, and gambling addiction, becoming an issue that can potentially touch almost every household in the country. Violence has always been a risk in some occupations, but in recent years it has become a present concern and danger for people who previously did not have to worry much about personal safety.

The first stage in dealing with anything is to try to understand the problem. Accordingly, each of these booklets begins with a discussion of the topic being addressed. For example, in the booklet on child sexual abuse, there is a discussion on the prevalence of child sexual abuse, the effects on victims, the different kinds of abuse and the characteristics of perpetrators. The topics covered in these booklets often lead to an instinctive withdrawal, or possibly revulsion. In attempting to understand the problem it is hoped that we begin to see the person who is the source of our problem not so much as a difficult (violent or abusive) person, but more as a person with difficulties. This has the advantage of releasing compassion and empathy, and encouraging us to engage strategies to help the person rather than simply label them as problematic.

The second stage is to ask what we can do about it. Each booklet has a section on how to respond, with the best available information about possible therapeutic approaches. There are also lists of 'do's' and 'don'ts' at the end of each booklet which may provide some practical advice on how to deal with the issue. At the end of the booklet you will find a reflection on what a Christian response might be to this particular problem. These are not exhaustive discussions, but are there to offer pointers which may help to illuminate and offer insight to the questions which can arise in a rather dark place. Those who are interested in a more developed discussion may benefit from reading Alan Bartlett's chapter on Practical Theology in *The Christian handbook of abuse, addiction and difficult behaviour.*

Each booklet contains a short section on care of self. This section has been written with leaders in mind. We realise that these booklets may be read by people who are not in leadership positions. It should not be difficult to make the necessary adjustments in order to apply the wise and practical advice offered in this section to your own situation. It has been included in each booklet as those who find themselves dealing with difficult and challenging situations can become stretched in terms of time, energy, relationships and personal resources. In order to help other people, you need to be in a healthy condition yourself. All of us have resources that enable us to rise to meet the challenges of a difficult situation, but, at the same time, very few of us can continue to manage without the support of others, and sensible choices that enable us to care for our selves.

We hope that you find this booklet informative, practical, insightful and helpful. If it provides an incentive to seek help, or information that enables you to understand better a difficult situation, or some thoughtful reflection on the issues involved, then we will have fulfilled our task.

Dealing with Difficult People

Jocelyn Bryan

Difficult people are those whose communication style and behaviour patterns serve to manipulate the behaviour and attitudes of others, causing them to feel inferior, threatened, intimidated or frustrated. They have a negative impact on organisations, lowering morale, creating confusion, reducing satisfaction, and impeding the efficiency and effectiveness of a team. People often leave a team or organisation because of the impact of such a person.

When I first worked in management it became apparent very quickly that the major challenges were not necessarily meeting targets and delivering client satisfaction, but managing the difficult people within the two teams for which I had overall responsibility. The most difficult of these was a team leader who was arrogant and aggressive. He always believed he was right and would not listen to others. He lacked sensitivity and self-awareness. When confronted with the effect of his behaviour on the effectiveness of the team, he became very aggressive and threatening. Another difficult person within the team was a friendly, sociable man who was always willing to take on any job you asked of him. Nothing was too much trouble and he was never resistant to anything. However, it became obvious that he was often unable to fulfil all the commitments he made. This was especially difficult when he was promising clients a service which he could not deliver. He had good intentions, but was unable to say 'no' to anyone. This was a source of frustration amongst both his colleagues and the clients for whom he had responsibility.

We have all encountered difficult people in various contexts and we are all, at times, 'difficult'. Being difficult is not a clinical condition but it can be on the borderline of personality disorder. Difficult people chronically use problematic behaviour and communication styles which have a negative effect on others and the effectiveness of any team or organisation they are part of.

I will explore some of these habitual behaviour patterns and suggest ways in which they might be modified and how others may cope with them. It also offers the opportunity for us to hold a mirror up to ourselves so that we might be more self-aware and attentive to the times when we become a difficult person. The psychology of anger is presented as a major explanatory tool in the understanding of these behavioural responses. This theme is developed further in the final section which seeks to explore how we can engage with anger theologically.

Introducing Jim, Sue and Mary

Jim

Jim has been passed over for a number of new opportunities in the organisation he works for. He carries the label of being a 'difficult person'. He works in a team but his colleagues do not experience him as a team player. Jim is often negative and critical in meetings, but this is expressed in an indirect way, for example in sarcastic humour. He makes asides, niggles and has a tendency to list reasons why change would be impractical or difficult. His attitude is negative but this is expressed indirectly. He is unwilling to volunteer to help other members of the team in new projects, but will do if asked. In such cases he accepts the responsibility willingly, but he is inwardly resistant and often misses the deadlines agreed and lets down others in the team. He is afraid of conflict and avoids any confrontations.

Sue

Sue is very involved with her church. She is a church steward and pastoral visitor, organises church bookings and is secretary of the pastoral committee. She works full time and has two children. Sue is friendly, responsive and always willing to do whatever anyone asks of her. She rarely disagrees with anyone and never confronts anyone, whatever their point of view or behaviour. She is very uncomfortable with conflict and often when there is a disagreement in church over who holds responsibility for a particular task, Sue will step in and take on the responsibility rather than let the situation lead to conflict. She is sociable and outgoing; most people would say they liked her. She therefore seems unlikely to be a difficult person to deal with. But she frequently makes unrealistic commitments and then lets people down. She makes promises in good faith but then is unable to keep them. The minutes of meetings are never circulated before the meeting and have to be tabled so members do not have time to give them sufficient attention. There is frequent confusion over who has booked the church premises for what, because Sue has promised it to two different groups at the same time, hoping she can please both parties and then not resolving the difficult situation she has created. Bookings are not recorded promptly or are sometimes inaccurate, so people feel frustrated and let down by her. She often can't attend the meetings she is required to be at, but doesn't let the church minister know until the last minute. She avoids sharing negative or difficult information, which leads to misunderstandings and a misrepresentation of the way things really are.

Mary

Mary also carries the label of being a 'difficult person'. She is described as forceful and often aggressive. Mary is impatient and when her plans are met with resistance or encounter obstacles, her impatience spills over and she becomes indignant and angry. She has a strong sense of what others ought to do and expresses this forcibly and with confidence. It is rare for Mary to acknowledge anyone else's skills or abilities verbally or

> in the manner in which she behaves. Mary is seen as hostile, condescending and sarcastic by her colleagues. She is prone to shouting at them and they find her behaviour and communication style intimidating. Mary is particularly difficult to manage as she is unable to receive feedback and shows little awareness of the impact of her attitude and behaviour on colleagues.

It is difficult to maintain positive relationships with these characters. Together, they represent the most challenging types of difficult people. There are obvious contrasts between them and hence they present very different challenges to those who are their colleagues or those who manage them. Jim and Sue show many of the characteristics of what has come to be labelled passive aggression. Jim disguises hostility by seeming to be nice. He might say he agrees with something but in reality he doesn't and this manifests itself in a lack of commitment and not following things through. He says what he thinks people want to hear and then expresses his actual thoughts and feelings in indirect comments. His words and behaviour are not consistent. He is difficult to deal with because he appears agreeable and compliant, yet his behaviour is problematic.

Sue is super-agreeable, which is often associated with passive-aggressive behaviour. She desperately needs to be liked and accepted. She is super-agreeable as a means of seeking and achieving approval, hence she does not express her actual thoughts, especially if they are contradictory. This means that she is not always honest. Like Jim, her words and actions are sometimes inconsistent. She over-commits herself because she fears saying 'no' will result in disapproval or negative feelings towards her and she always has a plausible excuse for her shortcomings. Many of her actions are rooted in her fear of conflict and disapproval. She frustrates those who work with her and is easily threatened when confronted with any criticism. Sue suffers from frequent headaches and has other symptoms related to stress. She believes it is 'unchristian' to express anger and that her role in the church community is to be 'nice' to everyone. Sue also fears expressing anger because this may result in others not liking her.

Mary, by comparison, behaves in ways which have been characterised as hostile-aggressive. Mary expresses her aggression and frustration openly and is hostile to those who disagree with her, challenge her or obstruct her in achieving her goals. This can express itself physically and verbally. She has to win. She is intimidating and powerful.

The common psychological feature of all three characters' behaviour is that they manage or mismanage their feelings of anger and aggression in such a way that their relationships with others are damaged or dysfunctional.

Bramson[1] describes difficult people as an ubiquitous phenomenon which has gone unnoticed and unexamined. It is evident that dealing with difficult people, whether they be colleagues, parishioners, clients or managers, is a frequent source of stress. Difficult people also present a problem to a team or organisation and can have a fundamental effect on the team or organisation's well-being and effectiveness. Bramson, as a management consultant, provides descriptions of the characteristics of 'difficult people' and how to cope with them. He describes a number of patterns of difficult behaviour which are categorised as the complainers, know-it-all experts, silent responsives, super-agreeables, indecisives and hostile-aggressives. He proposes that all these various behaviour patterns are motivated by a desire to gain control over other people.

In response to this analysis, the coping strategies he outlines focus on ways which enable the 'power balance' in the relationships with these people to be redressed and also minimise the impact of their behaviour on the immediate situation. A key factor in these strategies is acting with purpose and preparing possible responses to the difficult behaviour patterns. Evidently, it is necessary to ensure that the difficult person does not maintain control in the relationship, by using behaviour patterns which enable them to exploit others and exercise a destructive use of power. The effectiveness of coping strategies and also changing behaviour patterns depends largely on understanding the motivation for the difficult behaviour and factors which influence it.

Outline of approach

It is important to recognise what characterises difficult behaviour patterns and how they impact on other people and an organisation. These

1. Bramson, R. M. (1981). *Coping with Difficult People* (New York: Dell).

characteristics will be described in detail before the behaviour patterns are analysed. I will base my analysis on current psychological theories and use these to inform our understanding of the motives and factors which affect difficult people.

I have chosen Jim, Sue and Mary to serve as key examples. The main reason for this choice is the common psychological ground between them; namely anger and aggression. They also all have self-esteem issues and represent the three types of difficult people which people often report as being the most difficult to deal with.[1]

Difficult people are only experienced as difficult in the context of a relationship. It is the way they communicate with others and react to the situation they find themselves in that elicits the behaviour pattern that people find difficult to cope with. Their behaviour is interpreted and experienced as aggressive, negative, condescending, irrational, critical, abusive and frustrating. In other words, it is the way difficult people communicate and present themselves to others which is problematic. This is often accompanied by a lack of awareness regarding the impact of their behaviour on others and poor sensitivity and empathy. For this reason, any coping strategy must focus on how to manage the relationship and communicate with the difficult person in a way which allows thoughts and feelings to be dealt with sensitively and with respect. It requires good communication and listening skills.

There are many writers in managerial literature who make no attempt at this type of analysis. What they offer is a description of the behaviour and suggestions for coping strategies. In contrast, I want to suggest that by seeking to understand the difficult person's motives and the factors which influence these behaviour patterns, we can handle difficult relationships with greater insight and sensitivity, and increase the likelihood of achieving sustainable positive outcomes.

1. Anecdotal evidence: B. Geary.

Characteristics of difficult people

The identification of 'difficult people types' is well documented.[1] Here Jim, Sue and Mary's behaviour patterns are summarised.

Jim: Passive-aggressive

Key characteristics

- Desire for approval and general agreeableness
- Negative attitude and comments
- Subtle defiance
- Ambivalence towards most things
- Frequently uses misunderstandings, excessive demands, as excuses for their inefficiency
- Criticises others outside their presence
- Avoids conflict
- Sulks and refuses to discuss contentious issues
- Resistance to suggestions of others
- Lateness and forgetfulness
- Complaining
- Does not express anger or hostility
- Manipulative
- Procrastinates over decisions

Passive aggression describes a pattern of behaviour which carries a pervasive negative attitude. It is described as passive because there is normally little direct expression of resistance in interpersonal situations.

1. Bramson, R. M. (1981). *Coping with Difficult People* (New York: Dell); Brinkman, R. and Kirschner, R. (1994). *Dealing with People You Can't Stand* (New York, NY: McGraw-Hill); Keating, C. (1984). *Dealing with Difficult People: How you can come out on top of personality conflicts* (New York, NY: Paulist Press).

So the person complies with others in their demands or needs but is passively resistant to them and becomes increasingly hostile and aggressive as a consequence of this. The pattern of behaviour is understood as a defensive response leading to the avoidance of something the person fears. Often, this is fear of authority, competition, dependency, intimacy or conflict. A common expression of passive aggression is complying with the wishes of another and even committing to work to achieve these with enthusiasm, then failing to carry out the necessary task or action on time, or in a way which is unhelpful and puts the desired outcome in jeopardy.

In the past decade passive aggression has been recognised as a common syndrome. Examples of behaviours which fall into this category are agreeing to meet a friend for dinner at 7.15pm and arriving at 8.00pm, consistently failing to meet deadlines at work, being angry with someone and refusing to talk to them about it, always having a list of excuses for any shortcomings, agreeing to changes in procedures then gradually reinstating old ways of doing things. In daily life, in ministry and in occupational settings, passive aggression presents itself frequently, but by its very nature can be difficult to identify and deal with. It is a behaviour pattern which disguises underlying emotions.

Sperry[1] notes that passive-aggressive employees are relatively common in organisations but far less common in leaders. Interestingly, he goes on to comment that this is not the case in non-profit organisations such as religious communities, diocesan offices and non-profit making public-sector institutions where passive-aggression is a characteristic of leaders and employees and is associated with low morale and productivity.

Sue: Super-agreeable

Key characteristics

- Agrees with other's point of view
- Cheerful and socially outgoing
- Eager to volunteer
- Does not like to say 'no'

1. Sperry, L. (1990). 'Passive aggression in organisations', *Human Development*, 11 (2), 41–42.

- Over-commits
- Does not see things through
- Dislikes conflict and the expression of anger or discussion of anything unpleasant
- Makes promises in good faith
- Avoids confrontation whenever possible
- Fails to meet deadlines or is late
- Affirms others and makes them feel liked
- Never expresses anger
- Is negative about others when they are not present
- Minimises problems

Super-agreeable people are difficult to deal with because of their agreeableness. It has been suggested that the super-agreeable manipulates the presentation of reality to gain approval.[1] The fear of conflict and disapproval are significant factors in their behaviour patterns and this is undoubtedly linked to issues of self-esteem and the need for affirmation and acceptance by others. The expression of anger is often interpreted as a sign of weakness and lack of self-control and hence it becomes associated with fear of rejection and the lowering of self-esteem. This is especially apparent in church settings where cultures are created in which anger is often denied (and disapproved of) and conflict avoided. It is also the case that many churches are experiencing a decline in membership and there are more and more demands made on the existing members of the church community. Hence there is considerable pressure on individuals to be agreeable and take on additional responsibilities. This, coupled with the desire for approval as a Christian who lives out their discipleship in acts of service and puts others before themselves, makes super-agreeableness a problem in many churches. There are some obvious examples of how within

1. Bramson, R. M. (1981). *Coping with Difficult People* (New York: Dell), p. 90.

church communities passive aggression and super-agreeableness combine to result in a stagnant community where the psychological and spiritual well-being of both the people and the community is at risk.

The 'nice' church which is so fearful of conflict that it resists making any changes becomes stagnant and members drift away.

The parish priest who 'loves' everyone, agrees with everyone and is afraid to say 'no'. He is overworked, increasingly stressed and fails to meet his deadlines.

The church treasurer who grumbles to anyone who is willing to listen about the amount of money being wasted throughout the church, but never raises it as an issue in the finance committee meeting or makes suggestions to improve funding.

Mary: Hostile-aggressive

Key characteristics

- Impatience
- Abrupt and intimidating in interaction with others
- Needs to prove to themselves and others that they are right
- Presents as self-confident
- Aggressive and abrasive manner
- Lack of care for and trust in others
- Lacks capacity to receive and accept feedback
- Poor listening skills
- Lack of empathy
- Arrogant, with a strong sense of how others should think and act
- Lack of control of anger and frustration expressed verbally and sometimes physically

Hostile aggression is associated with a variety of characteristics as the list above illustrates. However, it is important to recognise that hostility and aggression are different, but that both are negative responses and inflict hurt, either physical or emotional, on another person. A person can be hostile but not aggressive, for example, by ignoring someone or being unresponsive to another. Emotional hurt can be inflicted intentionally without aggression being present. It is also the case that aggression can be an expression of caring for someone, or one might respond with aggression through indignation on behalf of a friend or relative. In the context of relationships, aggression and hostility are frequently expressed in response to conflict or a perceived threat and as such have a high emotional intensity. It is evident from the characteristics listed above that aggression in hostile-aggressive behaviour is a means of asserting power and establishing increased self-esteem. It seeks to intimidate the other person into submission or undermine or ridicule them or provoke them into a state of irrational anger. If an aggressive person holds a position of power within an organisation then they can be extremely difficult to deal with.

Jim, Sue and Mary's behaviour patterns reveal difficulties in their management of conflict, anger and aggression. When anger is not recognised or worked with constructively, it results in personal and social difficulties. Aggressive behaviour is often an expression of anger and frustration and manifests itself verbally and non-verbally in relationships. It is a response mediated through the sympathetic nervous system and the 'fight or flight' reaction stimulated by adrenalin. Hence, in the case of the behavioural characteristics such as those listed above, we are dealing with a universal innate human response which is being managed or mismanaged in the particular social setting and which is usually influenced by the personal goals of the individual.

Understanding aggression

These insights enable us to understand the nature of aggression and make it possible to understand not only our own aggressive tendencies but those of others. They also help us to develop strategies which enable us to manage relationships which are characterised by anger and aggression.

What factors influence aggressive behaviour and how does our expression of anger and aggression develop?

In Jim's case, his aggression and frustration is suppressed and then expressed in his negativity, sullenness, resentment and lack of commitment. Sue believes that if she shows her anger she will be rejected and it will damage the affirming relationships she desires, and so she disguises her anger and seeks alternative channels to express this. On the other hand, Mary's hostile-aggressive behaviour is an expression of her mismanagement of her aggressive feelings in her social context, and this leads to abrasive, angry, threatening and, in extreme instances, violent, physical behaviour. In each case, the mismanagement of aggression leads to relationships which are difficult and damage the social unit which they operate in.

Motivation for aggressive behaviour

Anderson and Bushman[1] see all aggression as including the intent to harm. However, they distinguish between hostile and instrumental aggression. Hostile aggression is defined as impulsive, driven by anger and motivated by the goal of harming the other.

It is conceived as being in response to a perceived provocation and is sometimes called *reactive* aggression. In contrast, *instrumental* aggression is seen as a premeditated means of obtaining a goal other than harming the other person. It is defined as *proactive.* A person may be verbally aggressive towards someone in order to bully them into supporting one of their proposals, but not to harm them as such.

Current theories of aggression

There are a number of different theories of aggression which help us to understand how aggressive behaviour develops and what influences it. These are outlined briefly below.

Social learning

Undoubtedly some people are more aggressive than others, but what determines this depends on how they have learned to express aggression and anger through their upbringing, observing others, and the beliefs and

1. Anderson, C. A. and Bushman, B. J. (2002). 'Human aggression', *Annual Review of Psychology* 53: 27–15.

expectations regarding social behaviour which they have been taught and exposed to. This draws on social learning theory which explains how we develop our understanding of the expectations of the social world we inhabit and behave accordingly. We observe and experience aggression in our early lives, and through these experiences and observations we learn when and how to express aggression in our social world. The key influences in this learning process are the observed aggressive behaviour patterns in families and other significant social settings such as school.[1]

Script theory

Heusmann[2] suggests that we store our experience and awareness of patterns of aggressive behaviour in what he calls 'aggressive scripts.' A script is defined as a well-established concept held in our memory which is essentially a set of connected actions linked to goals and likely outcomes. It contains causal links so that the relationship of 'If . . . then . . .' is programmed into the script. We hold scripts for numerous behaviour patterns ranging from catching a bus or eating in a restaurant to dealing with a distressed child. When behaviour patterns are well rehearsed or frequently repeated they are activated or accessed more easily. They also have a large number of links and associations connected to them in memory. This increases the chances of these behaviour patterns being activated across a number of situations. In this way the behaviour becomes generalised across a number of situations through the association network which it accumulates in the memory system.

This theory is particularly helpful in accounting for how a child who has frequently witnessed aggression in their parent's marriage as a means of establishing power and influence, acquires a script incorporating this pattern of behaviour which is then readily activated across many situations in their subsequent interpersonal and social relationships. So when the child can't get its own way in the playground, the script is activated and it behaves aggressively towards its peer group. The cue for activating the

1. Anderson, C. A. and Bushman, B. J. (2002). 'Human aggression,' *Annual Review of Psychology* 53:27–15
2. Heusmann, L. R. (1998). 'The role of social information processing and cognitive schema in the acquisition and maintenance of habitual aggression,' in Green, R. G. and Donnerstein, E. (Eds.), *Aggression: Theories, research and implications for policy* (New York: Academic).

script for aggressive behaviour is the child being obstructed in achieving its goal. Likewise, the child is more likely to throw a tantrum which includes physical violence towards its parents and teachers if it has frequently seen and experienced such outbursts as resulting in obtaining power and influence. Hence, a behaviour pattern of aggressive behaviour is evoked when they feel threatened or want to exert power and influence over someone or a particular situation.

Social interaction theory

Another theory which has significant explanatory power in this field is social interaction theory. This explains aggressive behaviour as a form of social influence behaviour. It suggests that aggression is used to produce changes in the behaviour of another person. This is particularly helpful in understanding our example of Mary as it begins to draw light on the motivation behind her aggressive behaviour. Aggression is seen as a coercive behaviour which is used to obtain something of value – for example, support for a proposal, money, help, goods – or to exact retribution and right a perceived wrong, or to build up a self-image or social identity of, for example, power, influence, competence. In this theory, aggressive behaviour is a set of premeditated actions directed towards achieving a desired outcome. Hence there is a reasoned goal motivating the aggression which could be anything from inflicting punishment on someone as negative reinforcement for a perceived provocation, to bolstering one's social image of being a tough person who is determined to achieve a particular end result.

Recent findings[1] suggest that aggression is often elicited by threats to high self-esteem, in particular in cases of unwarranted inflated self-esteem. The theory explains many aggressive behaviour patterns in teams and communities where aggressive behaviour is used as a means to enhance one's self-image and self-esteem.

An extension of this theory is related to parenting style. This has been used to explain the development of passive-aggressive behaviour patterns

1. Bushman, B. J. and Baumeister, R. F. (1998). 'Threatened egotism, narcissism, self-esteem and direct and displaced aggression: Does self-love or self-hate lead to violence?', *Journal of Personality and Social Psychology* 58:156–63.

which the individual uses to cope with either threatening, restrictive parenting or inconsistent parenting. In the case of inconsistent parenting, many of the characteristics of passive-aggressive behaviour – for example, indecisiveness and contradictory behaviour – were modelled by parents. The child then does not develop either the cognitive understanding or emotional maturity to assess what is expected of them socially or emotionally. This contradictory parenting style results in a lack of assertiveness and poor self-esteem in the child which continues into adulthood. The child becomes fearful of commitments, unable to predict confidently the responses of others, uncertain of their abilities and afraid of expressing emotions overtly. In parenting styles where the child's needs and desires are frustrated, the child may not risk losing attention or may fear possible rejection from expressing anger directly. Hence, the frustration and anger are expressed indirectly in negativity and resistance but at the same time maintaining compliance for fear of rejection.

Other factors to consider

Personality traits

Some people are predisposed to higher levels of aggression.

Sex

Males have a higher tendency to aggressive behaviour linked to their levels of testosterone. Males are more likely to express aggression directly, but females prefer indirect aggression. This may well be linked to gender differences in social learning, with parents and schools modelling and reinforcing different behaviour patterns of aggressive behaviour according to gender.

Beliefs

If a person believes that aggressive behaviour can lead to the outcome they desire, they are more likely to be aggressive in a given situation. However, if a person's faith tradition views aggression as negative and a sign of weakness or moral failure, then a person is less likely to express their aggression directly.

Provocation

This is probably the most significant single cause. This may include insults, criticism, thwarted plans. Baron,[1] studying workplace aggression, found perceived injustice as positively related to aggression in this context.

Frustration

When someone can't attain or obtain what they want they become frustrated. Sometimes this leads to aggressive behaviour towards the person who has been identified as responsible for the lack of goal attainment, but it is also the case that the target of the aggression may not be this person and the aggression is displaced and directed towards another person or organisation. In both Jim and Mary frustration is a key situational factor in the behaviour patterns shown.

Jim's aggression

In the case of Jim, a passive-aggressive, we can see how these factors combine to lead to some of the characteristics of his behaviour. Jim is frustrated in his work and feels undervalued and overlooked. He has an overwhelming need to be liked and avoids and resists any conflict. He is frustrated and angry about his position. His self-esteem is being lowered by his current situation. However, he believes that if he shows others in his organisation that he is angry about the number of opportunities for which he has been overlooked, he will risk damaging his chances for the future and face rejection or condemnation. Jim believes that showing aggression has a negative effect on relationships and seeks to exert social influence in other ways. Hence he expresses this anger and frustration indirectly by being inefficient, being negative and critical of others behind their backs and resistant to any new ideas. As is often the case with passive aggression, he may be unaware that these are expressions of his anger or of the damaging effect he is having on the organisation and his relationships within it.

1. Baron, R. A. (2002). 'Social and personal determinants of workplace aggression: Evidence for the impact of perceived injustice and the Type A behaviour pattern', *Aggressive Behaviour* 25:281–96, quoted in Anderson, C. A. and Bushman, B. J. (2002). 'Human aggression', *Annual Review of Psychology* 53:27-15.

Sue's aggression

The identification of how Sue manages her anger and aggression is more difficult, because they are avoided. Like Jim, she avoids conflict and she sees anger as a negative emotion. From social interaction theory Sue's behaviour can be understood as the repression of aggression helping her to achieve her desired outcome of maintaining affirming relationships and being accepted. Her motivation for repressing any feelings of anger is that she believes this would put her relationships at risk and in her understanding of social norms she believes that displays of anger are unacceptable and show lack of self-control and weakness. Hence, she is fearful of the consequences of expressing anger and the effect it will have on her relationships. From social learning theory the influence of Sue's parents' attitude towards the expression of feelings and the influence of her church background will also be affecting her behaviour. However, it is likely that Sue will be expressing aggression in ways she is unaware of. Some of her inefficiency may well be unintentional, but she excuses herself by listing the demands she is facing rather than learning to say 'no'. The same can be seen in her increasing tendency to be forgetful. Alongside this she might well become increasingly resentful about her workload for the church for which she receives little reward and no thanks! In addition her symptoms of stress may well be related to the repression of her anger.

Mary's aggression

Mary is a hostile-aggressive. We see some of the factors described above working out in her in a different behaviour pattern. Mary is motivated by proving herself and having power and influence in the team. It is important that she achieves her objectives and this is an important factor in her self-esteem. When others resist her ideas or plans, she becomes irritated and frustrated. Her self-esteem is threatened. To bolster her self-esteem she uses aggression to threaten others and achieve power over them in order to achieve her goals. She is forceful and self-confident. She does not listen to others and firmly believes she is right. Some of her anger she understands to be 'righteous anger'. In Mary's case this is a learned behaviour pattern which has a reasoned goal.

When Mary is thwarted or frustrated, her aggressive script is activated and she adopts the behaviour pattern which she has acquired through observation and experience.

Self-esteem

Another important psychological factor in each of our characters is their self-esteem.

Self-esteem is defined as an overall affective evaluation of one's own worth.[1] It is evident in each of our characters that their difficult behaviour patterns are related to their self-esteem. Branden,[2] in his book on how to raise your self-esteem, suggests that low self-esteem causes people to be less ambitious, less creative in their work and less likely to treat others respectfully. Furthermore, they are less likely to assume responsibility and will look for others to blame.[3]

Research using adolescents and college students found that low self-esteem was associated with a tendency to reject or be overly sensitive to criticism, an avoidance of making decisions and a resentment of being told what to do.[4] Hostile-aggressive behaviour is frequently elicited when criticism is voiced. The confrontational response and bullying behaviour of hostile-aggressives acts as a facade to hide the wound that criticism causes to an already low self-esteem. Their behaviour pattern may also include sarcasm, boasting, arrogance and over-estimating their abilities to appear superior. All of these are strategies to establish a sense of power or inflate their self-esteem.[5]

In the case of passive-aggressives, low self-esteem is expressed as a fear of being rejected or behaving inappropriately, so they procrastinate when

1. Balscovich, J. and Tamaka, J. (2001). 'Measures of self-esteem', in Robinson, J. P., Shaver, P. R., Wrightsman, L. S. (Eds), *Measures of Personality and Social Attitudes* (San Diego, C A: Academic Press), quoted in Rayens, B. L. (2001). 'Predicting difficult employees: The relationship between vocational interests, self-esteem and problem communication styles', *Applied H. R. M. Research*, 6 (1) 33-66.
2. Branden, N. (1988). *How to Raise Your Self-Esteem* (New York: Bantam Books).
3. Hamachek, D. E. (1987). *Encounters with Self* (New York: Holt, Rinehart and Winston).
4. Rosenberg, M. (1965). *Society and Adolescent Self-Image* (Princeton, NJ: Princeton University Press).
5. Rayens, B. L. (2001). 'Predicting difficult employees: The relationship between vocational interests, self-esteem and problem communication styles', *Applied H. R. M. Research*, 6 (1) 33-66 .

making decisions, they offer very little input in meetings, they may be negative and will not volunteer for any new responsibilities since they risk being disliked or rejected.

Super-agreeables classically fear rejection and have an overwhelming need to be accepted and affirmed. Their self-esteem is fragile and anything they perceive as potentially threatening to their relationships and their acceptance is resisted. They fear the consequences of saying 'no,' disagreeing with others and expressing their anger.

Whilst low self-esteem can manifest itself in difficult behaviour patterns, it is also the case that inflated self-esteem is associated with problematic behaviour, especially in communication and relationships. When someone with high self-esteem feels that their authority or competence is being threatened, they respond with an aggressive communication style. Individuals with high self-esteem make unrealistically positive claims about themselves.[1] Consequently, they set themselves unrealistic goals which can lead to failure. When failure threatens their egos, they compensate for their deflated self-esteem by using sarcasm and negative communication styles to intimidate others and make them appear inferior, thus restoring their feelings of superiority.

1. Baumeister, R. F., Heatherton, T. F. and Tice, D. M. (1994). *Losing Control: How and why people fail at self-regulation* (San Diego, CA: Academic Press).

How should it be dealt with?

Many of the people who we have so far considered do not have diagnosable personality disorders or suffer from mental illnesses (although this may sometimes be the case). While many people can benefit from therapy, it is not always necessary, nor will everyone be open to benefiting from this. There are, however, interventions that can be helpful.

Super-agreeables often need to learn how to be more assertive. They have difficulty saying 'no', and can create difficulties for themselves that can lead to frustration, resentment and feelings of not being appreciated. They can also benefit from group therapy where their avoidance of conflict and negative emotions will be challenged in a supportive setting. This can provide the corrective emotional experience that will give them greater resilience in interpersonal situations. Adjusting to new behaviours may lead to a period of clumsy interactions; however, after a period of time the super-agreeable, by learning their own limitations and respecting the boundaries of others, can become an asset to the church or organisation. Many church groups now provide training in conflict management and assertiveness to help clergy, volunteers or workers to deal with uncomfortable emotions, especially anger. There are also training agencies that provide similar training for therapists, psychologists, social workers and people in other work settings.

Passive-aggressives can be more difficult to help as so much of their energy is invested in avoidance and denial. They can also be helped by workshops on communications and assertiveness, although this may need to be supplemented by therapy that focuses on emotional expressiveness, as they have difficulty owning and articulating their own feelings. Group therapy can also be helpful for them. Irvin Yalom, who has worked extensively with psychotherapy groups, writes:

> Members of dynamic therapy groups, which have ground rules encouraging open feedback, may obtain considerable information about maladaptive social behaviour. A patient may, for example, learn about a disconcerting tendency to avoid looking at the

> person with whom he or she is conversing; about others' impressions of his or her haughty, regal attitude; or about a variety of other social habits that, unbeknownst to the patient, have been undermining social relationships. For individuals lacking intimate relationships, the group often represents the first opportunity for accurate interpersonal feedback.[1]

Passive-aggressives often require feedback in a safe setting in order to identify, understand and begin to change their behaviour. Individual therapy can also be helpful, but group therapy is probably more valuable and effective for people who behave in this way.

Aggressive individuals often resist any kind of help. However, they too can benefit from workshops on assertiveness and aggressiveness where they can see how their behaviour is affecting other people and experiment with new behaviours that enable them to get their needs met without trampling on the needs or feelings of others. They can also benefit from cognitive-behavioural therapy that helps them to reflect on their life goals and their values, and whether or not their behaviour is helping them to achieve what is important for themselves or the organisations they belong to. The comments made about group psychotherapy for passive-aggressive individuals also relate to aggressive people. They can benefit from receiving feedback in a safe setting. Other group members can be helped to give direct feedback which is often difficult – and difficult for the aggressive individual to hear – in social or work settings.

1. Yalom, I. D. (1995). *The Theory and Practice of Group Psychotherapy* (New York: Basic Books), p. 16.

A Christian response

I have suggested that the management of anger and aggression is a significant factor in the three types of difficult patterns of behaviour described. Anger is a powerful emotion which is often expressed in aggressive behaviour patterns. Within the Christian tradition, anger and aggression are responded to negatively. However, it was only in the nineteenth century that the psychological category of emotions was established. Prior to this time these psychological states were understood as passions and affections of the soul.

Passions were seen as signs of and punishment for the original sin of Adam and Eve. They were interpreted as manifestations of the disobedience to the will and were in tension with the affections of the soul which were viewed as the more refined, spiritual and aesthetic desires which drew the person towards beauty, truth and goodness.[1] Hence anger was understood as an emotion to be tamed, avoided, repressed or controlled. It was associated with sin, disobedience and failure. The challenge for the Christian Church over the past century has been to develop a response to emotions which is consistent with our understanding of the nature of God, of relationships and of our human nature created in the image of God in the light of our ever-increasing knowledge of human psychology.

Throughout psychology's history as an academic discipline, the complexity of our emotional landscape has challenged understanding and theory. Many conflicting and complex theories of emotions have been proposed, and these too have contributed to the confusion in the Church and the continued dominance of the historical negative interpretation of emotions such as anger, depression and anxiety.

The biblical narrative also presents a picture of contrasting and contradictory responses to the expression of anger. The New Testament gospel of Good News reveals the God of love, mercy and grace, whose sacrificial love for us led Jesus to the cross in loving obedience to his heavenly Father. But alongside this we have to place the anger of God portrayed in a dreadful destructiveness in the Old Testament.

1. Watts, F. (2002). *Psychology for Christian Ministry* (London: Routledge), p. 67.

There are over 400 references to God's anger in the Old Testament. Responses to this aspect of God's nature probe at the heart of our understanding of the very nature of God and how God interacts with his creation. One approach sees his anger as a reflection of his holiness and part of his relationship with humankind. Another emphasises the passionate nature of God where 'love is experienced not only as peaceful creativeness but as violent breakthrough.'[1] Jurgen Moltmann[2], a German theologian, develops this in his understanding of the suffering God, suggesting that 'love is the source and the basis of the possibility of the wrath of God . . . As injured love, the wrath of God is not something which is inflicted, but a divine suffering of evil.' Although this is appealing in the sense that it maintains the love of God as the central core of his being and at the same time does not deny God's anger, it falls short of explaining the divine destructiveness and terror which we find in some of the Old Testament texts.[3]

There remains a degree of mystery and unease in God's anger. Part of the challenge of our spiritual journey is not only to engage with and respond to God's grace in our lives but also to explore within our dynamic relationship with God how to live with the mystery of his being and active presence in creation.

The condemnation of expressed anger is echoed throughout the New Testament. Jesus in the Sermon on the Mount says, 'if you are angry with a brother or sister, you will be liable to judgement.'[4] Likewise Paul in the Letter to the Ephesians writes, 'Lead a life worthy of the calling to which you have been called, with all humility and gentleness, with patience, bearing with one another in love, making every effort to maintain the unity of the Spirit in a bond of peace.'[5] And later in this chapter he writes, 'Be angry and do not sin; do not let the sun go down on your anger.'[6] In this letter, the link between how we behave and our spirituality is clearly

1. Haughton, R. (1981). *The Passionate God* (London: Darton, Longman and Todd), quoted in Campbell, A. V. (1986). *The Gospel of Anger* (London: SPCK), p. 8.
2. Moltmann, J. (1974). *The Crucified God* (London: SCM), p. 272.
3. Campbell, A. V. (1986). *The Gospel of Anger* (London: SPCK).
4. Matthew 5:22
5. Ephesians 4:1-3
6. Ephesians 4:26

recognised. The Christians in Ephesus are instructed in this chapter to deal with anger appropriately. Paul quotes Psalm 4:4, saying that anger should not lead them to sinful behaviour. In other words, they need to manage their anger and deal with it before they sleep at night because if not, they are vulnerable to the devil. What you do when you are angry reflects your spirituality and the holiness of your living. We are called to Christian living which demands expressing our anger in ways which reflect the life and love of God. But the tendency to deplore human anger as sinful continues in Christian communities and this has a negative effect on both Church communities and the spiritual growth of individual Christians.

Yet, there are obvious examples of Jesus expressing anger. The memorable scene in the temple after his triumphal entry into Jerusalem, when Jesus overturned the tables of the money changers is arguably when his anger was most dramatically expressed.[1] Here we have a significant example of Jesus exhibiting a necessary expression of anger in response to the misuse of God's house, but its significance goes beyond this as it illustrates that anger can be justified in the face of abuse and injustice.

The acknowledgement of anger leading to a positive outcome goes back to early Christianity. Lactantius[2] in *The Wrath of God* makes the helpful distinction between righteous and sinful anger, but as Watts[3] notes, the acceptability of displays of anger was most likely dependent on the person's status in society. However, the distinction between different types of anger, and whether it can be either constructive or destructive depending on the circumstances, is found in much of the psychological literature.[4] There are many situations when anger can lead to positive developments in human relationships as well as the reversal of acts of injustice and exploitation. This demands a more positive and functional approach to anger. Righteous anger – anger expressed on behalf of others in response to situations of injustice, exploitation and victimisation, or in

1. Matthew 21:12, 13
2. Lactantius. 'The Wrath of God', in *The Fathers of the Church,* vol. 54, ed. Defarri, R. J. (Washington, DC: Catholic University of America), quoted in Watts, F. (1997). *Zygon,* 32 (2), p. 255.
3. Watts, F. (1997). *Zygon,* 32 (2), p. 255.
4. Bowlby, J. (1980). *Attachment and Loss, vol. 3. Loss, Sadness and Depression* (London: Hogarth Press); Fromm, E. (1973). *The Anatomy of Human Destructiveness* (New York: Holt, Rinehart and Winston).

personal situations when something significant is threatened – can be a catalyst for positive development in relationships and eventual outcomes.

The more people care about something or someone, the more likely they are to feel angry when situations lead to disappointment or frustration. Campbell[1] develops this and suggests that the closeness between anger and love can be approached creatively by considering how a loving anger might overcome both apathy and enmity. Anger is also ignited when a person's sense of vulnerability or inadequacy is touched. By reflecting on the circumstances in which anger is elicited, self-knowledge is increased and the emotion managed more appropriately. Any Christian response should therefore incorporate the adaptive nature of anger and its positive outcomes, as well as the negative effects of its expression, in its framework.

One of the most fruitful ways to proceed through this maze of contradictory understandings is by building on the distinction between the emotion or feeling of anger and its expression. Condemnation of the aggressive or passive-aggressive expression of anger which leads to physical or emotional hurt is a very different matter from condemnation of the emotion itself. This point was recognised earlier in the discussion of Ephesians chapter 4.

Anger is part of our daily lives and it has an effect on our health and well-being. Luther warns that without anger we might reach a state of oblivion where nothing changes and where in the end love itself loses all power. The way we deal with anger is connected with spirituality.[2] Spirituality is not something to be kept in our hearts but touches all of life including the words we speak and the way we relate to and interact with others. Many difficult pastoral situations arise through the use or abuse of anger. The confusion and uncertainty it gives rise to, both theologically and personally, causes many Christians to feel lost and lacking in confidence when dealing with it. Frequently the expression of anger is ignored or avoided. This view is supported by Fox[3] who observes that the avoidance of anger in Christian communities may remove justified anger

1. Campbell, A. V. (1986). *The Gospel of Anger* (London: SPCK), p. 95.
2. Ferder, F. (2000). *Words Made Flesh* (Ave Maria Press), p. 68.
3. Fox, M. (1979). *On Becoming a Musical Mystical Bear* (Philadelphia: Paulist Press).

from the centre of Christian prayer life. This leads to love of neighbour being confused with 'being nice'. Such 'niceness' can result in a number of negative effects in the ministry of pastoral care,[1] including negative feelings being repressed, the accumulation of resentment and a pattern of denial in relationships which engenders a culture of conflict suppression. Likewise, Campbell argues that while anger can be denied it cannot be eliminated from human life.[2] He suggests that the more we refuse to face it, the more it will undermine the possibilities of true Christian love through a cloying 'niceness' or ill-concealed resentment.

How can we respond to anger and the difficult behaviour patterns that arise from it in a way which is hopeful, positive and incorporates our understanding of the gospel and Christian living? An approach of personal re-education and management can lead to changes within the Christian community's approach to anger and passive aggression. This involves discovering the cause of personal anger, working with this constructively, avoiding both angry outbursts and any indirect expressions of the emotion. It also seeks to reduce the anxiety concerning the effect of expressing disagreement in relationships and looks to develop an approach which includes respect for self and others. This requires trust, honesty, and, to some extent, taking the risk of vulnerability with others. Recognising our anger, owning it, trying to understand it and communicating it constructively are envisaged as key stages in this process. Wicks claims that once Christians and religious communities stop seeing anger as being either good or bad and recognise it as a sign of personal vitality, they will be able to distinguish between experiencing the emotion and expressing it.[3] This is essential to managing anger constructively and eliminating the avoidance, passivity, denial and suppression which has led to difficult behaviour patterns in many individuals.

In leadership the inability to express personal anger or cope with the experience of anger in others can be a major factor in the avoidance of dealing with difficult people. In Christian leadership it is often the case

1. Augsburger, D. (1979). *Anger and Assertiveness in Pastoral Care* (Philadelphia: Fortress Press).
2. Campbell, A. V. (1986). *The Gospel of Anger* (London: SPCK), p. 94.
3. Wicks, R. J. (2004). 'A threat to Christian communities: Angry people acting passive aggressively', *Human Development* 25 (3) 8-16.

that shame is associated with personal feelings of anger and also with the discovery that the leader may elicit anger in others. As I have already illustrated, such responses can be the source of difficult behaviour patterns in leadership and organisations.

Dealing with difficult people is a necessary task in enabling the body of Christ to flourish and to fulfil its mission. For some Christians, to define another human being as difficult is to be judgemental and to show a lack of compassion and respect which is out of keeping with the commandment to love our neighbours as ourselves. However, it is undoubtedly the case that there are patterns of behaviour which are difficult to deal with and have a detrimental effect on relationships and the effective functioning of organisations. The mismanagement of anger is arguably one of the underlying causes of some of these common difficult behaviour patterns. By managing our own anger and the anger of others in constructive ways, the vitality encapsulated in this emotion can be directed positively towards building up the body of Christ for its service in the Church and the world. This depends on good methods of communication, empathetic listening and a more positive approach to our emotional life.

Do's and Don'ts

Dealing with difficult people

How do we manage these difficult people in ways which enable them to modify their behaviour patterns and improve the quality and effectiveness of their relationships?

Do's

- Do identify the behaviours which are presenting the problem and analyse these in more detail. What, when and how often? Is there a pattern?
- Do ask questions. Keep them simple: 'What makes you feel angry about what is happening in the project at present? I am aware that you have taken on this new project, but you already appear to be fully stretched with your other commitments. Would it be better to ask someone else to take on this project?' Asking questions of others in the team or organisation is also helpful.
- Do name the problem and listen to the response of the person concerned with empathy, asking gentle probing questions to uncover what the person is thinking and feeling.
- Do identify possible solutions. Identify a number of options to address the issue positively.
- Do follow through the chosen plan and monitor regularly.

The passive-aggressive

Do's

- Passive aggression arises out of the mismanagement of anger and aggression. It is repressed and hidden. To recognise it, it is helpful to be attentive to unexpected feelings of anger in ourselves and others. Passive aggression is covert and the person behaving in this way may not be sufficiently self-aware to realise the effect of their behaviour on others. They are trying to avoid being seen as aggressive even though they feel negative and angry about something.

- Empathise and probe gently. What makes the passive-aggressive angry? Within the relationship encourage the discussion of feelings in a non-judgemental way. Build up trust in the relationship.
- Attend to inconsistencies between their actions and words. Give them feedback and probe what this might suggest about their feelings.
- Affirm assertive behaviour. They are frustrated and annoyed and they cannot express this in an appropriate manner. Affirming their assertiveness encourages them to express their emotions and thoughts and reduces their fear of being judged negatively for doing so.
- Manage your own expectations of their efficiency and inability to complete tasks. Work with them to set realistic achievable goals which can be reviewed regularly. This will increase their self-esteem through the achievement of goals and reduce your feelings of frustration with the passive-aggressive.

Don'ts

- Don't agree with their complaints and negative comments but do listen to them.
- Don't be afraid at times to interrupt, especially if you are having difficulty controlling the structure of the conversation.

The super-agreeable

Do's

- Reassurance of personal acceptance and respect for their honest opinions will encourage trust and openness within the relationship. The super-agreeable has low self-esteem and is fearful of conflict and disapproval. The more accepted and affirmed the super-agreeable feels, the more likely they are to be honest about their feelings and limitations.

- Affirm assertive behaviour. Conflict avoidance is a controlling factor in their behaviour pattern, so the affirmation of assertiveness and saying 'no' to requests will enable them to manage their commitments more realistically.
- Be clear with them on priorities and help them plan their commitments.

Don'ts

- Don't allow them to make unrealistic commitments.
- Don't allow tension and disagreement to escalate. When tension increases they are more likely to agree to things they can not achieve.

The hostile-aggressive

Do's

- Give them some time to 'calm' down.
- Listen and try to ascertain what the cause of conflict/frustration is, and how they are feeling about it. It is also necessary to be able to express your feelings. Good listening skills and the ability to express yourself well are important in resolving a problem involving hostile-aggressive behaviour.
- Draw attention to the way you are being treated without becoming hostile.
- Share how you feel but do not attack the person.
- Watch the non-verbal expression of anger and control. If they have not sat down, encourage them to do so.
- Maintain eye contact.
- Be empathetic and try to establish the facts.
- Stand up to the hostile-aggressive without fighting![1]

1. Bramson, R. M. (1981). *Coping with Difficult People* (New York: Dell), p. 25.

Don'ts

- Don't attack the person.
- Don't worry about always being polite – you may need to interrupt.
- Don't argue with what they say or try to demean them.

Conclusion

Difficult people are encountered throughout all organisations. I have already examined three types which are commonly cited as the most testing to manage: passive-aggressive, hostile-aggressive and super-agreeable. These all share difficulties with handling anger, conflict and aggression. I have suggested that the psychological understanding of anger and aggression provides useful insight into analysing these difficult behaviour patterns and developing coping strategies to work constructively with the emotional response which is elicited.

There is confusion and avoidance surrounding anger and its expression in the Christian tradition. This has led to Christian communities failing to deal with difficult people and sometimes to a cloying niceness and lack of growth. This has been explored in the discussion of a Christian response. Many theological questions arise from this, but I have sought to focus on our response. The question of God's anger, to name but one, has received grossly inadequate attention. What is abundantly clear is that when anger is elicited, it will be expressed. How it is expressed can determine whether the outcome results in a difficult behaviour pattern or not. The consequences of the management of this potent emotion can damage relationships and the effectiveness of an organisation. The way in which anger is expressed by an individual has been shown to be influenced by a number of interacting factors including parenting style and self-esteem. Dealing with anger requires recognising our own anger, the positive function of anger and how it can be used constructively in relationships and organisations.

Recommended reading

- Bramson, R. M. (1981). *Coping with Difficult People* (New York: Dell).
- Campbell, A. V. (1986). *The Gospel of Anger* (London: SPCK).
- Keating, C. (1984). *Dealing with Difficult People: How you can come out on top of personality conflicts* (New York: Paulist Press).

Caring for Yourself

Alison Moore

Introduction

Being involved in a difficult situation as it unfolds is demanding and challenging. It is possible that you are *at this moment* caught up in the kind of situation described in this booklet, and this section is written with you in mind. Among all that can be said about how to take care of yourself as well as those for whom you may be responsible, there are three particularly important points to remember:

- Self-care is important for good leadership and management;
- Self-care is to do with the whole self;
- Self-care usually needs help from someone else.

If you do not have the energy or motivation to read this section, then **please give it to a colleague or friend**, who can read it with you in mind and point you to any parts that might be helpful to you. This part of the booklet is divided into four sections:

- Self-care and normal reactions.
- Ways of approaching sensible self-care.
- A Christian response to the idea of self-care.
- Practical suggestions.

What does self-care look like?

Current phrases like 'work-life balance' imply that we should be leading well-balanced lives. While striving to live 'balanced' lives, it is important to bear in mind that as Christians we are primarily called to be disciples, made in the image of our complex, vibrant God. This calling involves recognising the significance of both the physical and spiritual aspects of our lives. A healthy spirituality involves living our humanity to the full. This means that we live in and through our physiological and our psychological make-up and therefore, when exposed to the stress of a difficult situation, this is where we feel the consequences. Showing the strain does not mean that God doesn't love us, nor that we have been an inadequate Christian.

What is self-care?

Care of self is to do with the whole self

Care of self applies to our physical, mental, emotional, behavioural and spiritual experiences, which are interrelated. For example:

> If you eat too much sugar (*behavioural*), you will crave more (*physical*), and you will think you need more chocolate (*mental*). So you will eat another bar (*behavioural*) and feel guilty (*mental / emotional / spiritual*).
>
> If in a religious service you have a sense of God's love and purpose for you (*spiritual*), your anxiety decreases (*emotional*) and your knotted stomach relaxes (*physical*).

Sensible self-care recognises the links and makes allowances.

Care of self is to do with long-term ways of living

We are physically designed to alternate between stress and rest, tension and relaxation. People who do only one or the other lose touch with their humanity. If a rubber band is left permanently stretched, it will stop working and be thrown away. It lasts longest if it is stored in relaxed mode until needed. Like rubber bands, most people can stretch to function well under stress, and we are designed to do just that. However, when we habitually override the need to rest, we reach a point where we can no longer relax, mentally, emotionally, spiritually, behaviourally or physically.[1]

Care of self will look different in different people

We can be surprised that other people's ways of self-care are different from our own. Introverts withdraw, extroverts seek company; some people are energised by activity, others by tranquillity; some need strenuous physical exercise to clear the mind, others need sleep. Forgetting this, we often try to follow someone else's good advice, rather than trust our own instinct about what we need; or we suggest in vain what will help another.

Care of self is essential for good leadership and management

Managers, like rubber bands, can become useless if habitually overstretched. This can show in different ways:

physically, in exhaustion, sleeplessness, appetite change, minor or major illness;

emotionally, in numbness, extreme or inappropriate reactions, inability to notice or respond to others, or to receive feedback;

mentally, in skewed thought patterns and illogical approaches, inability to assess situations or to recognise this;

behaviourally, by excessive drinking, caffeine intake, extremes of sexual activity, obsession with detail, longer but less productive hours, anger outbursts, irregular eating patterns;

spiritually, by avoiding prayer or only praying for miracles, superficial external religious compliance, excessive sense of responsibility and with it guilt that refuses compassion, emphasising some Christian themes more than others, ignoring failure as a route to new possibilities, acting out of pride disguised as responsibility.

1. See Sarah Horsman's helpful work on stress reactions described in Litchfield, K. (2006). *Tend My Flock* (Canterbury Press). See particularly chapter 4 sections 4.28 – 4.31.

People, especially leaders, who are overstressed, are not good for their organisations or for the people they are responsible for. Standards of good practice demand enough self-awareness for competency. As a wise person, you will look out for debilitating signs of stress in yourself, and **ask someone else to keep alert too**.

Normal responses to a difficult situation

Normal initial responses to shock[2]

The term '*shock*' sums up the collection of initial reactions in a difficult situation. As the *whole self* will be affected, physical sensations, behaviours, thoughts and feelings may all be different from normal and fluctuate.

Shock reactions are normal and there for good reason. With a limited amount of energy available, it is as if parts of us 'freeze' temporarily so that other parts can function well. Some of what is frozen will later thaw when there is opportunity, and strong emotions or physical exhaustion can surprise long after the difficult situation is over.

Many people experience shock positively, with adrenalin leading to clarity, decisiveness and more energy than normal. However, too much adrenalin can paralyse thinking processes. Also, because you think you are functioning well, you are less likely to realise when you are not doing so. If others trust you as a competent person, they are unlikely to question your behaviour now. Unwise decisions and difficult consequences can follow.

In the early days of a difficult situation your *role* as leader will be affected as people have greater expectations of you. They will expect you to function competently as normal; to manage the unfolding situation in a wise way; to anticipate and meet the needs of those you are responsible for. You may not meet these expectations.

Your *relationships* too will be affected. As manager, your performance is the focus of other people's interest, advice and quite possibly criticism. During difficult situations, misunderstandings can flourish, and relationships suffer. You can find yourself becoming a different sort of leader from the sort you thought you were.

2. There are many good descriptions of responses to sudden loss. Any book on bereavement will cover this, e.g. Worden, J. W. (2001). *Grief Counselling and Grief Therapy* (Third edition), (Bruner-Routledge). For more detail about shock responses, see the chapter 'Caring for Yourself' in Geary, B. and Bryan, J. (eds) (2008). *The Christian Handbook of Abuse, Addiction and Difficult Behaviour* (Kevin Mayhew Ltd).

In church contexts, the divide between work and personal relationships can be much less clear than in other work situations. Church members may not see the need for your changed role as you manage this unusual situation.

The difficult situation may take a lot of time, and will certainly drain your energy. Home relationships may be robust enough to accommodate a period when you are preoccupied. However, if there are ongoing demands there too (young baby, flatmate in crisis, bereavement, teenagers . . .), you might need to explain your limited responses.

Normal mid- to longer-term responses to shock

Once a situation has been dealt with and life is back to normal, the relief can lead us to believe prematurely that we are quite back to normal ourselves. As our perception may still be out of sorts, we may not notice how much we are still affected.

Also at this stage the delayed emotional and physical reactions from the initial 'shock' phase can kick in, bringing waves of tiredness. Even two or three years after a seriously difficult situation, a loss of confidence can still be felt.

The impact on *role* and *relationships* is going to be just as strong, but possibly less obvious than at the start. Perhaps your situation simply cannot be resolved, so that instead of your usual role as 'fixer', you have to develop a new role of 'container'. Others in the organisation are likely to forget that the leader is still affected by the ongoing effects of the situation (for example, complicated confidentiality issues may remain). Relationships can change as a result.

What does 'normal' mean for me?

My 'normal' is likely to be different from yours, not just because of our different situations, but also because our individual reactions will differ depending on our personality and how we usually function.[3]

3. The Gilmore Fraleigh 'Style Profile' work is easily accessible and makes a useful distinction between typical reactions when life is calm and when it is stormy. See, for example, Gilmore, S. K. and Fraleigh, P. W. (2004). *Style Profile for Communication at Work* (USA: Friendly Press). The Mennonite Centre in London has a good book service. www.metanoiabooks.org.uk

Approaching self-care

As you face this difficult situation, particularly if you are a manager or leader, some of the following are likely to be true:

- you experience a loss of control – of your diary if nothing else
- you are on a steep learning curve – this may be the first time you have dealt with anything like this
- your overall workload increases – your 'day job' still needs you
- you need to be extra alert – as you might be operating at the edge of your competency
- you need to reflect but there is little opportunity for this – but everyone still expects you to act wisely
- you are bound to fail – to make the *right* decisions at the *right* time in the *right* way for everyone.

However pressurised you feel as you face this difficult situation, it makes sense to step back briefly. By assessing, or 'mapping,' both the situation and yourself you will make a better job of leadership.

Mapping the situation

Assessing the demands of the difficult situation and the resources available[4]

It helps to be clear where the lines of responsibility lie between the people involved, both inside and outside your organisation. Clarity about role is useful too. You might need to have different roles, possibly incompatible, at different times and in different relationships. Churches in particular are often unclear organisations, with a volunteering culture that can take good practice for granted rather than setting out clear guidelines. Methodically answering the following questions, preferably with someone else's help,

4. For more detailed suggestions of structured ways of mapping the elements of the situation see the chapter 'Caring for Yourself' in Geary, B. and Bryan, J. (eds) (2008). *The Christian Handbook of Abuse, Addiction and Difficult Behaviour* (Kevin Mayhew Ltd).

will clarify your role and responsibility:

- *Who* and *what* are being affected by this situation?
- What are the *needs* of each person or project?
- *Whose responsibility* is it to meet each of these?

You should now be able to see two things clearly:

Which needs are *not* being met.

Where *your* responsibilities lie.

This in turn will remind you who needs to be briefed about what, what you need from senior management and what support you can offer to junior colleagues.

The Drama Triangle

This schematic way of analysing situations can be very helpful when you are trying to map a difficult situation, particularly when things seem stuck, or you find yourself responding in ways you are not happy with. As its name suggests, the 'drama triangle' looks at the role people *actually* find themselves playing rather than the role they *think* they are taking.

Without realising it, people slip into one of the three positions shown in the drama triangle, '**persecutor**', '**rescuer**' or '**victim**'. They then find that they are thinking and feeling just what the named role suggests. The added difficulty is that the roles can quickly swap round. If you can spot which role you are playing, you are well on the way to being able to do something positive about it.

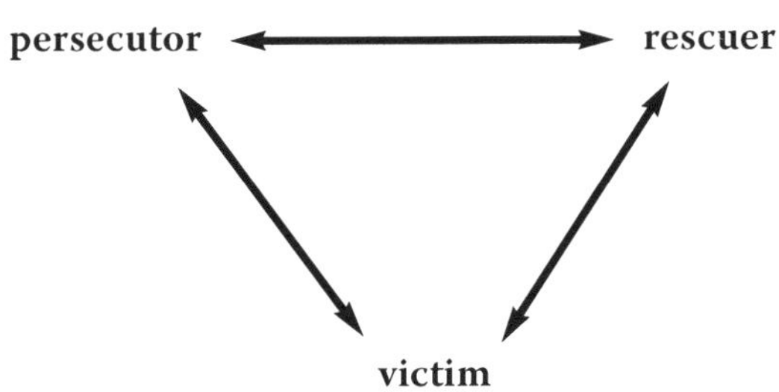

- When you are in '**victim**' role, you act as if you do not have the resources to solve the problem, you feel without thinking;
- when '**rescuer**' you take too much responsibility for someone else and ignore your own needs;
- as '**persecutor**' you are absorbed in your own needs and disregard others.

To change this into a 'winners' triangle' one of the three players must stop trying to change the others and concentrate on changing their own behaviour. The 'winners' triangle' shows how each player can make a change:[5]

- the **victim** can become **vulnerable** i.e. you recognise the strong feelings, but think about how to get help to do something about it;
- the **rescuer** can become **caring** i.e. you show concern and offer help, but within your own limits and without taking over;
- the **persecutor** can become **assertive** i.e. you find ways of meeting your own needs, but without disregarding others.

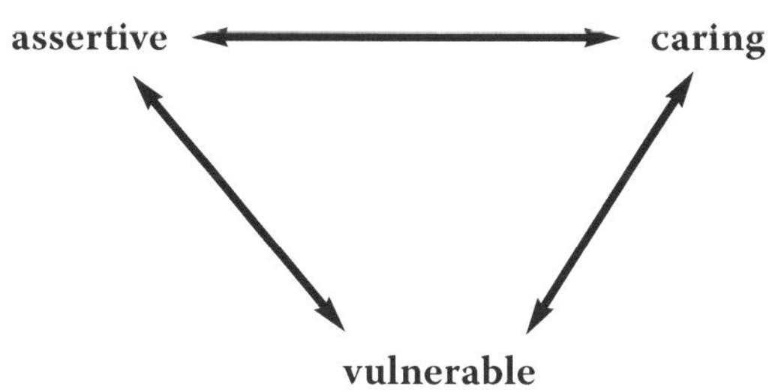

5. For a worked example of the drama/winner triangle see the chapter 'Caring for Yourself' in Geary, B. and Bryan, J. (eds) (2008). *The Christian Handbook of Abuse, Addiction and Difficult Behaviour* (Kevin Mayhew Ltd).

Mapping yourself

Personality

It is useful to know how you function under normal and stressful conditions, and what resources *you* need to work best. You might already be familiar with this through a personality-typing theory.[6] If you are not sure what you are normally like, especially when in a leadership role, or whether you change under stress, just ask a friend or colleague what they have noticed.

This can help you and those around you to make sure that you access the right sort of resources in a difficult situation. What you need might not be obvious to you or those around you. It helps, too, to know what you want from others when you are in stress conditions. For example, do you prefer to delegate or retain control, prefer company or solitude, helpful suggestions or silence? If everyone has realistic expectations then many crossed wires (and cross exchanges) can be avoided.

Relevant past experiences

If you have gone through difficult situations before, you will bring the learning from that into the present. Reflecting on how you responded can help, because even if the current *situation* is completely different, your instinctive *reaction* might be the same. If that reaction worked well, you can trust yourself to act the same way now. But if it did not, you will want to think about how to do things differently this time. For example, if your instinct in a previous difficult situation was to plough through alone and this led to a breakdown of health, you will need this time to act against your instinct and make sure you enlist support.

Even minor past experiences that we are unaware of can impact on the present. When the *dynamic* in a current situation is similar to something we have experienced previously, we can *react* in a similar way. For example, Jill's teenage years were full of conflict with her father whom she saw as domineering and dogmatic. Now a junior minister in a large church, she often argues with her senior male colleague.

6. Most familiar are Myers-Briggs Type Indicator and the Enneagram. Gilmore Fraleigh is more concerned with communication styles than personality.

Relevant current experiences

The dynamic of current experiences can also have an impact, with significant events in your private life affecting how you experience the current difficult situation. This is like a kind of subterranean crossover, experienced emotionally rather than rationally. For example, Val was surprised at the vehement rage she felt towards her team member who had been arrested, accused of financial irregularities. A friend pointed out that it was only six months since Val's husband had left her for someone else, clearing their joint account as he went.

Outside help

The goal of self-care is to manage our lives and work in such a way that seeking outside help when appropriate is simply a normal part of how we live. It is sensible to identify someone you can talk to, for example a friend, line-manager, supervisor or spiritual director, when you need to vent, explore options, or reflect on how you have handled a problem.

Non-managerial supervision

Many people in ministry and other professions with a strong people focus are making use of what counsellors have practised for years – non-managerial supervision, or 'consultative support'. This is a relationship where you can reflect in a structured way on work issues and their impact on you. This benefits both you and your workplace.

Coaching

Coaching is a relatively new area. Working with a coach can help to improve work-life balance, identify goals for development, and explore aspects of yourself that block progress. Although you are unlikely to embark on a coaching relationship while in the midst of a difficult situation, you could use it later to process your experience.

Burnout

Many individuals who work in the caring professions, especially those with responsibility for management, can suffer from burnout. Burnout happens slowly, involving emotional exhaustion with a slow erosion of spirit, loss of idealism and lack of belief that your contribution makes any difference.[7] In common with other stress reactions described earlier, burnout can be obvious to everyone except the person suffering it. For someone already near burnout, having to manage a difficult situation can be the last straw. Treatment for someone in this situation will involve consulting a GP, probably followed by time off work, and individual and/or group therapy.

7. Loudon, S. H. and Francis, L. J. (2003). *The Naked Parish Priest* (London: Continuum).

A Christian response

Christians have mixed reactions to the idea of 'self-care', thinking that the biblical evidence 'take up your cross, lay down your life etc.' mostly argues against it. Many loving Christians encourage others to care for self, while patently not applying this to themselves. Even those who really believe in it can find it difficult to live it in our multi-demanding society.

Of course, we are promised strength beyond what seems humanly possible, and many Christians will testify to this. But this doesn't shortcut the reality that we are physical and psychological human beings. We are still likely to feel deep exhaustion after a challenging set of circumstances, however upheld we were during them. When Elijah fled for his life and wanted to die, God met him in the profound spiritual experience of the 'still small voice' and sent him back to recruit Elisha. But first he had to regain his strength with plenty of sleep and food.[8]

While it is true that self-denial is an important part of Christian discipleship, it is also true that at the heart of Christian faith is the promise of full and joyful living. This is life lived in proper perspective, acknowledging that power, wisdom and love are sourced in God, seen and claimed in Christ and experienced through the Spirit. The joyful Christian disciple takes in as well as giving out, reflects as well as acts. The second commandment is 'Love your neighbour *as yourself*.' This carries a wise psychological insight, that how we treat ourselves is linked with how we are able to treat others.

In other words 'self-care' is *not* the same as 'selfish'.

8. See 1 Kings 19:1-18

Practical suggestions

This section is set out as lists of suggestions so that you can see quickly what might be relevant to you or someone you know. There is some overlap between the lists.

Be realistic

- Life will be different for a while with the inevitable invasiveness of the situation.
- You will be tired and sleep might be broken.
- Eating patterns might change.
- Using stimulants to keep going or alcohol to relax can help *but* ask someone to alert you if you are becoming dependent on them.
- Emotions may well fluctuate more than your normal pattern.
- Prayer may be affected, so ask someone trustworthy to pray on your behalf.
- Normal habits and routines might not work.

Remember

- The big picture – what has God called you to and what do you value most in life?
- If possible do some of what normally helps to keep you sane.
- Stay in touch with people and writings that are good, particularly if there is evil and violence involved.
- Keep your world bigger than the difficult situation[9] – children are useful here.

9. Jerusha Hull McCormack describes this in her book *Grieving – A Beginner's Guide* (Darton, Longman and Todd, 2006). Instead of waiting for the grief – or, in this case, the difficult situation – to diminish in order to have space in life for other things, she suggests deliberately enlarging your world so that the grief or difficult situation does not completely fill it.

- Be creative, even for half an hour, by giving your full attention to music, sport, weeding, DIY ...
- Humour and laughter can vent the most difficult of emotions.
- Routine, not necessarily daily, can help.
- Self-awareness and self-regulation will stand you in good stead.
- Symbolic 'cut-off' points can keep the situation separate from personal life, e.g. a change of clothes or a particular prayer.

Be sensible

- Avoid email communication whenever possible, as the 'send' button cannot be cancelled.
- Delegate, for example by asking someone else to be spokesperson.
- Prioritise, asking for help if you cannot see how to do this.
- Check your opinions and decisions with someone whose judgement you trust.
- Find allies who can help protect you and others from your limitations.

Find support

- Identifying personal support is a sign of strength, not weakness.
- If support from senior personnel is lacking, consider requesting it or explore other options.
- Colleagues and staff might need suggestions for how best to support you.
- Family and friends' ideas of support may be different from yours, so check.

If the difficult situation is in the public arena

- Check that you are using all the resources that are available to you.
- Be on your guard when with other professionals, as the needs of those caught up in the situation can get disregarded in the agendas of the 'experts.'
- Take advice before responding to the media and give yourself time by saying, 'I'll ring you back in ten minutes.'
- Be resigned to the fact that you can't exit from the public arena.
- Stick to your own particular role.
- Know who is responsible for the victim, the perpetrator, the organisation, the other people in the organisation.
- Expect misunderstanding and criticism.

Do I talk about it?

- Some talk is essential – you need someone to be a sounding board.
- Some talk is optional – offloading on someone outside the situation.
- Communication inside and outside the organisation needs careful thought.
- Give yourself time to think by always using the answerphone.
- Conserve emotional energy by giving brief answers when asked about the situation. 'It's very challenging,' 'I am fairly exhausted,' 'We're doing what we can.' Don't go into detail.
- Check with your partner if and how you will talk about it at home. Talk late at night or in your bedroom can be particularly invasive.

If the difficult situation is in a church context

- Although you are the minister, remember that you are not God.
- Although you know you are not God, remember that others will expect you to be.

Listen to your whole self

- Whatever your inner emotions and thoughts, maintain a 'non-anxious presence'[10] for others by breathing deeply, and deliberately relaxing muscles that are tense.
- Notice what you are thinking and what you are feeling.
- Aches in your body will give you clues about the stress you are carrying. Recognising their existence will help.
- Acknowledge the discomfort of conflicting emotions and thoughts.
- Be kind to yourself rather than blaming yourself.
- Stay connected – with yourself and with others.
- Be prepared for the long haul – this is likely to take longer than you anticipate.
- Emotional energy drains physical energy.
- Look for a way of processing the experience later when there's opportunity.

Conclusion

Far from being self-indulgent, self-care is both necessary and godly and a certain amount of self-awareness is helpful. Even under pressure it is worth taking a step back, with the help of someone else, to assess both the situation and yourself. Dealing with a difficult situation will probably take

10. This phrase is used to describe what a mediator offers in conflict transformation work. It provides a succinct summary of what a good leader can offer during a difficult situation.

more out of you than you would think possible – emotionally, physically, mentally and spiritually. Make allowances for a recovery period when the repercussions will go on making an impact.

When you hold a managerial or leadership role you owe it to your staff, colleagues or congregations as well as to yourself, your family and friends, to look after yourself enough to be competent and safe. If this applies to the daily challenge of finding a Christian path in our multi-demanding organisations, it surely applies even more when we face an out-of-the-ordinary difficult situation.

Further reading

- Dr Ruth Fowke has written very accessible short books that look at the issues of stress and Christian faith e.g. *The Last Straw* (Eagle, 2000).
- Daniel Goleman's *Emotional Intelligence* (Bloomsbury, 1996) is the classic on the importance of taking whole-person responses seriously.
- Robert J. Wicks has written a book for counsellors and mental health professionals entitled *The Resilient Counsellor* (Oxford University Press, 2008). It contains wise advice for all managers and clergy who find themselves in stressful situations.
- For those working in churches and other Christian organisations, the Alban Institute, an American publisher, has an excellent range of books on 'practical knowledge in leadership and congregational life.' www.alban.org/bookstore